HAIL AND FAREWELL

HAIL AND FAREWELL

Abby E. Murray

perugia
PRESS

FLORENCE, MASSACHUSETTS
2019

Perugia Press extends deeply felt thanks to the many individuals whose generosity made the publication of *Hail and Farewell* possible. Perugia Press is a tax-exempt, nonprofit 501(c)(3) corporation publishing first and second books of poetry by women. To make a tax-deductible donation, please contact us directly or visit our website.

Book design by Rebecca Olander and Jeff Potter

Author photograph by Jenny L. Miller

Cover art by Meredith Bergmann, 2001: "Response to Random Murder I: September 11, 2001, New York City, 2,996 dead," 18" × 10" × 12" (bronze, edition of 9).

Cover art photograph by John Bigelow Taylor

Artist note: "The image of the woman came to me when I was thinking about the Houris, the virgins who were supposed to be waiting for the terrorists in Paradise, and what a travesty that idea made of all that is truly feminine. I imagined them being greeted by this woman, instead: a human being who has survived and absorbed an attack."

Artist website: meredithbergmann.com

Library of Congress Cataloging-in-Publication Data

Names: Murray, Abby E., author.
Title: Hail and farewell / by Abby E. Murray.
Description: Florence, Massachusetts : Perugia Press, [2019]
Identifiers: LCCN 2019021349 | ISBN 9780997807639 (pbk.)
Classification: LCC PS3613.U7565 A6 2019 | DDC 811/.6--dc23
LC record available at https://lccn.loc.gov/2019021349

Perugia Press
PO Box 60364
Florence, MA 01062
editor@perugiapress.com
perugiapress.org
perugiapress.com

for military spouses who see what happens during and after war,
especially those still searching for their way to speak

CONTENTS

Three

ONE

FIVE DAYS AFTER THE WEDDING

Five days after the wedding
we go down to the harbor
and draft your living will,
have my picture taken and printed
on an army ID card.
I wear a purple silk dress and earrings,
straighten my hair and leave my book in the car,
still too giddy to know where I'm going
and protest, tell the lawyer
I want nothing to do with the war
as if that is his business,
identifying pacifist wives
and sending them home with good wishes,
without funeral plans for their husbands
or Red Cross magnets
or a sheet of paper that says
What Happens after Death in Combat.
My thumbnail cuts the arm
of my wooden chair when he asks
if you prefer to be buried with brothers in arms.
Everyone keeps saying *God forbid.*
You pull a stack of papers I didn't notice
from between your arm and rib cage,
a cupboard I hadn't counted,
and I watch your finger
trace pages of charts and numbers.
I ace my signature
and the lawyer calls me a champ.
When I leave my teeth hurt
like I've been at the dentist's office,
like I've sat for hours with a clamp on my jaw.
I look down at my new ID

and see the younger version of myself
sitting in front of white butcher paper,
happy to be so close to the ocean,
her belly still full of lemon cake and champagne.

CROSSING THE KNIK

We move to Alaska and wear
each other's clothes,
just married, sharing t-shirts
and pullovers and boots.
We are pre-war together,
us before Iraq:
your last name stitched in black
onto field green duffel bags,
my father's name following me
like a good cat into the den
of officers' wives.
We bring the charcoal
barbecue inside when a moose
gives birth in the backyard,
half-sleeping while her calves
trample blueberries
on legs like bedposts.
The Knik River floods
beneath the bridge to Palmer,
ice running below us in shapes
the way clouds might:
a camel, a star, a rocket.
Look at us, you in the driver's seat
and me beside you, both of us
hunched into ourselves like bears,
still lucky and warm and new.

RANGER SCHOOL GRADUATION

A cadence is written like so:
wives show up for the mock battle
at Ranger School graduation
in heels and spandex skirts,
some of us threaded into silk thongs
and some bare-assed,
some in black and gold
I ♥ My Ranger panties,
all of us too late
to hear this morning's march:
You can tell an Army Ranger by his wife!
You can tell an Army Ranger by his wife!
Because she works at Applebee's
and she's always on her knees,
you can tell an Army Ranger by his wife!
Look, we sway like choirgirls.
When you're paraded into the lot
beside Victory Pond I pretend to know
which smudge of red is you.
Already I am washing your uniform, your back.
Your mother says *oh, oh!*
and claps: the sound of deer ticks
kissing your blistered necks
before we can.

WEDDING MARCH

Here are the spangled white folding chairs,
most of the battalion and their wives, a few kids.
Friends, we gather here to celebrate
the survival of a man who returned from war
not once but three times. Get a good look
at his lapel, a future filled with stars.

We honor his willingness to love
despite the Bronze Star he carries down the aisle,
his weeping mother on the crook of his arm.
There is a bride. Her father conquered a gulch in Vietnam
and favors the hip still burdened by his sword.
The sun sets yellow over a sensible kiss.

This is how we welcome our newest wife:
our husbands swat her on the ass with sabers
as she is guided down the aisle toward
endless cosmopolitans at the open bar
and a new name squatting on her signature
like a forty-pound cake.

TOM CALLS FROM BAGHDAD

here

                  and

     anti-aircraft

so

                corkscrew

     see what

burning

         told me

smoke   are

women, hiding

        know

           a bike

   we

them

        it's okay

looking   tires

       walls   maybe

to cook

you

      this phone

          letters

BONES

written at the hospital bedside of Specialist Kegley,
wounded soldier of the 1-501st Infantry Battalion

To watch the explosion in slow motion
would expose the human body more fully,
its loyalty to the mind even when divided
by shards of copper and hot steel:
crescent moons and teardrops of shrapnel
spiraling up the leg from ankle to groin like
morning glories curling round a fencepost.

Two of them shear the calf muscles whole
from tibia and fibula while the last
splits the thigh to a burnt red canyon
deep enough to expose the wincing femur.
To see the torso, arms, neck, and head still whole
and know messages are rocketing down
from the brain, spilling from the wounds: *run*

and the bones below obey, bending and extending
without tendons or muscles, without flesh, acting
on the memory of nerves as it fades, the hollow echo
of commands demanding the bones *move,*
carry the body to safety, until the brain itself slows,
stops the messages and falls forward, the bones
still obedient, lying down in the sand.

BETWEEN JOBS

Employment recedes like the tide
and my daily life is exposed:
all I want is my Indian neighbor
to wave from his porch chair,
invite me to meet the parakeets
he keeps in a white wicker cage.
Every morning I wave
and wave like a trained seal,
supposing he is blind,
supposing he cannot see me
but would if he could.
The parakeets stare at my cat
who sleeps in the yard, belly up,
dumb as a dandelion.
My hope is monstrous.
There is nothing left to unpack.

REARVIEW MIRROR

I see my German shepherd in the back seat,
ears at attention, eyes filled with the ash of glaucoma,
and my two cats bundled like bread in their cages.
They are piled around my plastic suitcase,
two milk jugs filled with water, and a book.
The rear window frames a forest fire
as it seeps through the skin of Colorado.
It is so close I can make out the shapes of single flames,
one like an egret, its throat full of angles,
one like a turkey's wishbone.
The town is crisp, white, and afraid,
mostly ahead of me in traffic, heading east,
already missing what has yet to be burned.
Ten minutes ago I chose one book,
only room for one: Raymond Carver's poems,
with one about salmon that jump from the river at night
then swim into town, jiggle doorknobs
and disturb the peace. The first time I read it
I thought it had been written by my dad,
a toolmaker from Tacoma who died alone in his duplex.
The poem is short and doesn't try to be strange.
A psychiatrist once told me Carver's salmon
were figments of the Freudian unconscious
and my dad's greasy fingerprint disappeared.
The spine of the book has cracked
from my constant rechecking. If he comes back,
it will be just as a wildfire licks up my driveway,
right when I'm running my first red light.

POPPIES

They haven't bloomed yet in this photograph
of the farm which is not a farm:
an acre of soil patching the mountains
of Afghanistan and Pakistan together.
My husband writes to explain
how poppies are planted to look casual
and untended, blossoms sorted by tools
that mimic the wind and borders staked out
kilometers away above rocky cliffs,
borders made of men and children and eyes
and shouting: the ancient, original border.
Tom smiles in the photo, knowing
we will search the scene for fences,
for black-eyed blooms or proof of danger
lurking nearby, a pistol extended
from some nearby brush
or the glint of metal behind a rock.
His interpreter stands beside him
and gazes just left of the camera,
his face unworried and unimpressed.
Tom says he is a man of words, not things.
Poppies, yellow cliffs, cameras, uniforms,
he knows the words for each. He knows
several words for me, too: *lady, wife, American,*
domestic creature who writes letters,
identifier of poppies only when they are red
and conspicuous, not pinkish brown
and sleepy-looking, taught to look thirsty.

THE WAR TRAMPLES US

Upstairs, my neighbor reads
about carbon monoxide.
We communicate without language
at the shared mailbox
where we wait for letters
shipped in crates from Iraq.
When I say nothing to her
she says nothing back.

The floorboards groan
when she rocks her two boys
into a deep sleep, an ocean of night.
She floats to the garage, curls up
on the backseat of her Jeep
and tracks the brown moths
crawling across fluorescent lights.
They drop like folded paper.

Later, a man in fire gear
delivers her to my porch.
He says we should evacuate.
She apologizes, her voice
the hollow boom of babies
carried off in an ambulance.
What can I do?
I lean against the doorframe,
smelling poison.

NOTIFICATION

This is how I imagine it:

A black Durango follows me to work,
then home, tracks me to King Soopers
where I buy peppermint tea and milk.

It idles in the parking lot,
the driver obscured by clouds
of bitter exhaust. I know it is a man
by his shoulders, his grinding jaw.

I know he has drawn the short stick.

He tracks me home and waits
until the faint clicking of our luck
slows and stops. He steps outside
on a current of aftershave
and starched polyester, pulls another
man in uniform from the backseat:
he will stay to help me make arrangements.

They use the handrail on the wooden porch.
They expect to be wounded.

GWEN STEFANI KNOWS HOW
TO GET EVERYTHING I WANT

It takes a misdelivered *Cosmo*
to finally understand what I want
and how to get it. Gwen Stefani
tells the truth on page 89.
We believe in Gwen because
her apron of chain-link stars
sparkles over a black bustier;
star-spangled bondage, says an editor.
She slouches, holds the heel
of her right white Louboutin
in one hand as if to say Congress
respects my body, as if to say
rifles aren't worth shooting.
This is what I want and Gwen
is here to deliver. When she slips
into a red sport coat and jeans
she comes in loud and clear:
grant proposals that write themselves,
cartons of baby formula
sold from unlocked shelves at CVS,
eight days of rain over California.
Because Gwen knows how to get
everything I want, she can afford
to be an optimist. Pharrell is rad,
her mom is rad, the whole world
is rad. I agree, Gwen, I do!
And I'd be giddy too in that baby blue
jacket, its faux-bullet spikes screaming
peace talks and pacifism,
bubblegum fingernails that tell me
soldiers who drop my writing class

are only on vacation. She pulls
her Union Jack sunglasses down
with one finger. This means Ruth Stone
never died but went into hiding,
it means the grocery store lobsters
have escaped, it means I can refinance.
Gwen steps into a pair of fishnets
as if to say the 2nd Infantry Division
won't return to Iraq, as if to say minke whales
are singing on the Japanese coast.

SKIN LADY

The skin lady sells otter, moose, bear, and deer hides
on the corner of Northern Lights Boulevard and Seward Highway,
beginning in September all the way through first thaw.
As a community we have more sympathy for her than the man

who sells whale baleen on the same corner during summer,
who smiles into our open car windows and waves in his bare hands
enormous, bristle-edged fronds. The skin lady, whose face I have never seen,
whose face is the memory of a hood cinched around the scarf-drawn mouth,

keeps her hands layered in as many mittens as she can find in gutters
or lost in parking lots, whose hands I imagine are carved from wood.
I have never seen her with her arms at her sides. They sway above her head,
furs hanging down and filling with wind, as if to call their spirits back.

She keeps extra skins in a pile by her boots, heaped on the snow and salt.
I have never seen her set up shop or roll the furs back up at night,
and I've never seen a customer. In April, she disappears and Anchorage
is at its ugliest, all of us so sick of slush we barely remember a woman

selling skins on the corner so recently, a woman we only guess is female
because we can't make out the shape of her body, and the way
she returns each year makes us feel terrible about some crime
we know we've committed.

R & R

I'm on the stoop of our rented cabin
with a bag of peanuts
watching bats dip low
over the Cheakamus.
They are full of confidence
and crumpled caddisflies,
a late, unlucky hatch.
We've camped here before,
paid a hundred dollars
to pretend cabin 3 is ours,
the potbelly stove, ours,
the trout lamp and saltshaker, ours.
No letterbox, no cat tree,
no sewer bill clipped to the fridge.
We keep our voices low,
American English clanging
against our throats like a collar.
Cabin 2 thinks we are dirtbags.
You say you're proud
to be American but later,
at the community campfire
with the Swiss engineer
and a contractor from Kamloops,
you develop a French accent.
You call your R & R *vacation*.
You never leave a war behind.
Instead of sleeping,
we put our toes in the river
that reeks of death,
the end of a pink salmon run
and the survivors are rotting.
They wait in clouds of yellow foam
below submerged boulders
for the perfect time to jump.

A PORTABLE WIFE

Portable as a jug of water,
easy to lift, easy to set down
and sweet as a tissue-paper bookmark,
the way I hold my husband's place
when wartime calls. I dog-ear
my relationships with women
more efficiently than a sailor,
keep them calling for a week or two
after I leave town, my address book
ballooning in the shoebox like a mushroom.
I teach violin lessons from home,
set up shop and tear it down in minutes,
beat my hand against my thigh
while students I'll know till Christmas
pull horsehair over metal.
I serve beer to men who gather
the bones of their friends
like splintered glass, let their wives
compare my maiden name
to a wound I should allow to heal.
I donate furniture and clothes
with the coolness of a monk,
cram scraps of my childhood into a bin
that slides under the bed.
I check my reflection at night
to make sure creases are forming
where a good wife might find wrinkles,
tell myself I can fold my body up
like a wedding tent and be unrolled
again in a matter of hours.

I AM STRUCK BY GUILT

In formal receiving lines
I remove my satin gloves
by pulling each fingertip

and begging the Virgin Mary
not to let this commander
hear the screeching

I imagine in my ear canal:
the harpy I keep feeding there
so she'll come back,

her voice like a blister,
the rash of her feathers.
Pride makes her spit.

Small medals make her
want to roll in fire
and I am all she has.

The gloves take ages
to pull from my skin.

JEWELRY

I am bribed with jewelry to behave.
My wrists clink against the table.
My fingers catch on the backs of chairs
and my neck glitters with guilt.
A white gold bracelet of braided light
lures me to another military ball
where Captain Stanley hacks the cork
from a champagne bottle with his saber
and accidentally fills his wife's forearm
with shattered bits of glass.
I chase the emerald pieces
as if I've earned them, hustle Mrs. Stanley
to the bathroom and pinch each gem
with the silver tweezers of my Swiss Army knife,
patch her up with Band-Aids from my wallet.
This is how I remain calm.
This is how I lodge a complaint.
I rub despair into the amethyst on my knuckle,
name every shade of green in a pearl necklace
and pray the rosary into a Swarovski knot:
one shiny rock for every night the phone doesn't ring,
every close call, every care package,
a clasp on the end of every year.
My initials shine in lapis lazuli,
my pinky is wrapped in platinum.
I want to protest the diamond band
you order from Afghanistan, the heft
and glare of each stone that says
there is no more, your body is the final prize,
carved from the earth and polished.

ARMY BALL

You've outgrown the prom,
the men I mean, not us, the wives,
who spend hours buffing time
from our skin and dazzle
in pearls and tennis bracelets
clipped like medals to our bodies:
the OIF amethyst, OEF diamond studs,
SFAT cashmere, reintegration pearls.
Some new wives miss the mark,
overshoot the dress code
and show up in wedding gowns.
They pick at the crystals, the ruching.
At our table, your jaw is softened by gin
and lost time, that year before Iraq
when Blackhawks dropped you
into the unarmed mountains of Alaska,
a simulated war with its certain end.
The colonel's wife talks to me
about her family law practice,
eight years untouched now
on account of her boys and the traveling.
I want to hug her but we've just met
and I know she is being kind.
I'm wearing polyester, faux-leather mules,
pinned my hair up in the car.
We are saved by shushing
for the grog ritual: men of different ranks
come forward with liquor bottles so large
they represent entire wars:
dark rum for the jungles of Vietnam,
canned beer for Afghanistan.
A bowl the size of a bus tire is filled

with two hundred years of symbolic booze
and we hoot and clap when the men
take long drags from each bottle or can,
we scream as if to say the weapons burn
in our throats the way they do in theirs.
Waiters come round with pitchers
and serve grog with silver ladles
polished last night, too early,
tarnish blooming in their grooves.

TWO

PRAYER ON NATIONAL CHILDFREE DAY

Blessed are the miscarriages,
the midnight cramps
and ultrasound jelly,
the long tongue of photographs
that betrays my empty pocket.
Blessed are the minus signs
and skipped cycles and scarring,
the injections drawn up at dawn
by faithful partners
then needled into the thigh.
Blessed be the benders,
the cigarettes and sushi,
the labradoodles and collies
with a bed in every room.
Blessed are the scholars,
the babysitters and aunts,
for you shall bring us
the pregnant woman's confession:
her passion for pineapple
and your own wasted time,
her blue hour longer than yours,
her well of love dug deeper.
Blessed are the poems
you scratch into the ground,
the nights drained of sleep
and washed with worry.
Happy National Day of Choice,
Day of Desire, Day of Emptiness,
happy National Day of Solitude.
Happy Day of Nobody's Business,
happy Day of the Naked Night.
I've made a cake for you
nine layers high. Come,
bring a fork, bring a plate.

TO THE LOST CHILD

The doctor, a man in desert camouflage
and a badge clipped to his collar,
said he could find no trace of you.
He wasn't sorry. He looked and looked.
From then on, we spoke of you
the way good people talk about strays.

When I was a girl my kitten disappeared
and my father told me cats prefer to die alone
when it is time, they lie down in the woods
and dissolve with the mushrooms and bugs.
I was taught not to argue, to be graceful.

The day I lost you, child, my first, your father
brought me home and put me to bed,
my face white as a bowl of milk,
hands on my stomach, your empty room.

SEX IN A SMALL TOWN

When I was thirteen sex was a natural disaster
that never traveled far enough northwest
to reach my neighborhood, pressed flat
the way we were beneath Canada's belt.
Sex was an earthquake that buckled buildings
in southern California or a funnel cloud
that wrung Kansas out like a sponge.
It flooded the East Coast or froze cows solid
in the Midwest, it left everyone out of work
and tired-looking on the front page of our *Herald,*
which we read when asked to study current events:
Lorena Bobbitt, a woman whose name
made my teacher cross his legs under the table,
made him say sex was a madwoman's handgun,
or Bill Clinton, a man my mom called *smooth,*
and the woman who curled up under his desk like a puppy.
Sex was something that flooded other towns
and sank quietly into our wells, wholly invisible
but brutal. I knew it involved the pelvic area.
When I was ten I nailed scraps of plywood
to the trunk of an enormous cedar tree,
improvising a ladder toward the top branches,
and I thought about sex while I worked,
how I wouldn't spend that much time
listening to boys let alone exploring their bodies.
On a scale of boredom, sex was somewhere
between a board game and electrocution,
an event imported from adulthood
for people who no longer climbed trees.
In seventh grade, Amber Pulanski
slipped into first period English late
and said cum tastes like sugar mixed with water,

and after she explained what cum was
I reassured her: *come* is a verb.
It did not occur to me that sex could be sweet
or worth the way it might make a woman feel.
It could be, I thought, like the children
of hurricane victims, who build new schools,
stone fountains, and public gardens
then call their loss an inspiration.

HAIL AND FAREWELL

Each time you are issued new orders
your current duty station hosts a Hail and Farewell:
the ceremony during which you receive a plaque
and I am given a rose in a plastic tube.
You make a short speech, your commander calls me
by your last name and rank, then we eat pub food
for the last time with the battalion as if we are family.
Every year, my colleagues ask what this means,
my friends whose jobs hail them by issuing paychecks
and say goodbye by letting them leave. Last year,
we were hailed in a tavern basement in Scranton
and last night we were farewelled at a brewery:
the colonel made small talk with you and the major
and the major's wife sitting beside me. None of you
could believe the way Iraqis live on a lake of oil,
yet their power is cabled or trucked in from Iran.
When I tell my coworkers about the plaque
you received, still propped like a tombstone in my trunk,
I am not embarrassed to explain how you said
before accepting it, *I love the Iraqis,* and you meant it.
You love the translators who unknot your English
then weave it into fabric village elders can use,
love the small girl with her hand on a donkey's ear,
love the man who shares his chai, shows you
how to fold bread around a stew of tomato and meat.
Last night the major held up his left index finger,
made a circle with his right fingers and thumb,
miming crosshairs aimed at the waitress
and said, *Only one kind of Iraqi I love.*
I tell my coworkers about the tavern,
about my wilted rose in its airless container.
I tell them the wives are harmless, the way we sip
margaritas from pint glasses and say nothing
when our husbands discuss the ones they love.

WHEN HE RECEIVES ORDERS TO AFGHANISTAN
AND A PARKING TICKET: HOW TO RESPOND

What you say matters,
each word tagged
and monitored
like an eaglet.

Make your voice a small bird,
the kind he can hold
in the palm of his hand:
chickadee, sparrow, canary.

Use words that behave
in the corridors of memory.
Don't say *Fuck*.
Don't be a blue jay.

Don't crack your head
on the window
or rifle through his duffel.
Don't ask where he parked.

When he hands you the ticket,
its charges printed in dark red
script, let the checkbook fly
from your purse like a finch.

Post payment immediately
and sing, sing, sing.
Don't hoard bits of paper,
don't shred his orders.

Don't bark, don't pick.
You are not a magpie,
you are not a crow.
Your voice is a long, sweet song.

Build a nest
on his shoulder and rest
your head there.
Fill his ears with feathers

so downy and slight
they can flood a canal
and never weigh more
than an ounce.

POEM FOR MY DOG

Say you skip breakfast
and sometime around 3 o'clock
a friend asks how you feel.
In English, you are hungry
but in German you *have* hunger.
I learned this when emptiness
was a flavor I knew best:
a fruit meant to be roasted.
Now, in January, I stand
at my front window with coffee
and watch heat escape from the shadow
of our chimney on the snow.
I like to think I'm warming
a magpie's nest somewhere
while my dog sleeps by the stairs,
dissolving in a bone cancer
no science can tame.
She is hollowing herself
from the inside out.
We're alone so I explain to her
the difference between
being and having.
One language says
I am empty and one says
emptiness is mine.
She has no use for learning now.
I tell her, this year,
I will be given so much.

POEM FOR UGLY PEOPLE

Only we are not supposed to know we are ugly.
We are supposed to think you're talking
about the person standing beside us
at the coffee cart or in the elevator,
at the grocery store, squeezing peaches.

Always the ugly people are behind you,
the ones you don't see but can easily identify,
whose skin tags are tick-shaped
and hang from the cheekbones of women
who learned in first-grade classrooms
how to spell the word *beautiful*
and pictured themselves as they wrote it,
slinging grey loops of pencil around those vowels
we can't differentiate when we hear them:
beautiful, then *ugly,* with its trusty noise
like gum on the tongue and familiar,
every syllable spelled the way it sounds.

We learn what ugly is right before we learn
that seeing it on the face of a friend
makes us cruel, long before we understand
the body is a wrapper tightly twisted
around the impenetrable thing it carries.

Ugly people of the world, I want you to know
that without us there would be no perfect breasts
or the shallow dip of a man's collarbone.
Without us there would be no statues parading
in bronze through parks or even the smell
of sunlight on cedar. When my sister's first boyfriend
called me an ugly cow I wish I'd had the sense

to tell him without me he'd never see a cardinal
in winter and know it was a wonderful thing,
the way it preens like a beating heart
in the blackened plum and we shield our eyes
from the glare of the snow to watch.

SHORTLY BEFORE THE WORLD ENDED

Pain was still relevant.
Drugstores sold Tylenol,
Aloe vera, and bug spray,
they sold moleskin patches
and pregnancy tests,
wrapping paper and cards.
It didn't seem silly,
not to the customers
who filled their gas tanks
en route to addiction meetings,
company barbeques,
offices, and the gym.
They bought pre-paid phones
for conversations
they wouldn't have
and saved up vacation days.
They watered down the scotch,
chose broccoli over bread,
and slept in their clothes.
They promised their children
camping trips another time
because another time
was still relevant.
They misinterpreted,
as usual, the trees heaped
with swooning doves,
foxes trotting freely
down sidewalks like dogs,
dairy cows trampling
barbed fences into nearby fields,
ones with shallow creeks
sinking through ruts in the grass.

WHY WOMEN WRITE POEMS FOR THEIR SONS

America is ripe with a glut of boys—so many
they fill up our kitchens like ants
and carry bread away in their jaws.

Our highways flood with boys
who spill into rivers, displace female trout
and leave grizzlies snapping at air.

Women write poems for their sons
because the mountain range outside
is a pile of boys stacked one upon the other,

snow gleaming on their backsides,
trees like wet green arrows
leaning toward their open mouths.

Women write poems for their sons
because there is nowhere else to put them,
buildings burst at the rafters with boys.

We don't know where they belong
with their plastic dinosaurs and slingshots
and swords, their pocketknives,

bullhorns, recliners, and scotch.
Mothers approach blank paper
while boys tumble from laundry sacks

and slide down banisters into the ink
where daughters must be mined in darkness
if they are to be found at all.

We send canaries into poems, don't worry—
they return with girls' voices
in their beaks. Our boys turn into men

who promise empty spaces for our sons.
Someone suggests the open desert
and you can hear us consider it carefully

under the sound of boys bubbling in teapots
and hopping from our toasters.
Across the street, a pipe bursts.

Even the woman who whispers a prayer
for her daughter writes a poem for her son.

POEM FOR PREGNANT WOMEN WHO
HOLD THEIR STOMACHS IN PICTURES

I assume you know
the abdomen is secured
by muscle and tissue
to the good bone of your back,
that your unborn
has belted itself
like a mute copilot
into your center of gravity.
I assume you know
the womb is a moon
that pulls your own blood
toward the unknowable
but has yet to tumble
from its orbit
like the discarded engine
of some rocket,
here, in the middle
of a family photograph
where you seem
to hold it in place
like a ship that might
launch at any time
in a cloud of orange flames,
or like it is an offering
of fullness in a landscape
of empty altars.
I assume you know
we also look at stars,
those of us who bear
the peace of a moonless night
into each evening,

those of us who can
identify constellations
by their myth.
Isn't deep space
where the gods put women
to protect them?
Were they really better off
up there, burning
with voices we only hear
once they're spent?
I assume you know
we've noticed you,
pregnant women,
one hand cupped
beneath the belly,
the other on a lover's back.
What I'm trying to say
is that we see you,
we believe you have
a world's worth of climates
to carry more or less alone,
and what I'm trying to say
is that your arms
must be exhausted,
always lifting
some other person
into the frame.

HOMECOMING

Homecoming is the smell   of floor wax,
     artificial fog   pumped from a plastic tank
beneath the bleachers.   Every tour ends
in the same plume of white: a gymnasium
slung with regimental crests   and butcher
paper,   women in stilettos at two-thirty
in the morning   and babies in car seats
next to posters that say *Nice to meet you, Dad!*
            The man with a megaphone tells us
when your plane lands,   when you board
the shuttle,   when you're parked outside.
Women   sing battle carols to pass the time
            and in every song   America is a girl
so holy   even I want   to defend her.
     When you're just behind the double doors,
     my palms catch fire.   I half expect
     to look down   and see the flame of fear
blazing on my skin: you are   home
and I am burning   from the inside out.
The fog machine lurches   in its shackles.
Someone screams when you march through
the mist   with a hundred other men,
build formation,   every mouth a closed seam,
every neck a plucked chicken   squeezed
by the collar of camouflage.
We wait   until the man with a megaphone
finishes a prayer, asks for applause, then says
Ladies, find your soldiers! I cannot seem to locate
my feet   but my hands have begun to smoke,
     two scrolling signals   that reach
for the ceiling and spell   *find me, find me.*

ODE TO NORTEÑO

There is a kind of embarrassment
you remember without feeling sick:
that time we lived across the street
from a Mexican family who sold
produce from a UHaul by day
and blasted norteño in the yard all night.

It was Tuesday, because all that is good
and right is obscured on Tuesday.
We were drowning in the nightly news:
more of your friends dead overseas,
a helicopter driven into the desert floor
like a tent peg, women begging for food
with toddlers in their arms.
And the platoon of accordions
that rumbled over the street
shook the standing water of our sorrow.

We decided to cross the street together
and ask for lower volume, that was all,
though we intended to slouch into our hips
to make it clear how exhausted we were,
how much we deserved to hear the news
over their music, that we had earned
the sound of a white man's report.

When we opened the backyard fence
everyone turned to see who'd arrived.
A teenager, the one who drove the UHaul,
wheeled the volume knob counterclockwise
with his thumb. The air over their yard was cooler
than the air over ours, the grass

beneath their pecan trees like the ocean at night
while the yellow lawn below our dogwoods
lay brittle and smashed by the heat.
Pear-shaped light bulbs shed gold light
on the laps and foreheads and paper plates
of the family as if Christ had been there seconds before.
The screen door slapped and a woman yelled
inside the house, *Felix! Two plates!*
The call of our back-peddling.

We saw ourselves unmoored
in the gilded glow of summer,
our lives like burning boats.

We said we'd come to buy vegetables.
They gave us some peppers and a fat tomato
and when we offered to pay they put their hands up,
palms toward us, because they knew
it wasn't a quiet street we wanted
so much as knowing how to cross one.
We carried the vegetables home in our hands,
considered chopping them into a salad
then ate them whole with salt instead.

HOW TO BE MARRIED AFTER IRAQ

They schedule a reintegration conference
at the Doubletree two weeks after we pick you up
from the Fort Carson gym, your rifles oiled
and the dead weight of armor locked up
behind chain-link. For two weeks we reintegrate
our mouths and hands because there isn't much to say
after twelve months of letters. We forget
there is a colonel until his wife calls to tell us
the conference is mandatory, *ladies included.*
In the hotel ballroom, a chaplain introduces
two volunteers: husband and wife, here to demonstrate
how to be married after Iraq. He says we can
use the alphabet to identify a healthy marriage.
The couple stands side by side and bends
away from each other, their arms up like goal posts.
The chaplain says *this is a V*: this couple is growing apart,
pushing the other away by choosing different paths.
He has them demonstrate the letter *A*: a codependent pair
leaning forehead to forehead. They tremble from the effort.
A woman sitting in front of me draws a strike
through the letter *A* on a notepad. Finally, the right choice
for officers and their wives, a letter *H*: two people
clasping hands across a comfortable lunging distance,
their spines pointed straight up to heaven.
They are balanced and the chaplain tells them to smile.
He sends us home with a workbook
and a phone number to report domestic violence.
I fold the book in half and use it to scrape snow off the car
then take you home to practice the letter *S*, the *Y*, the *L*.

MEMORIAL DAY

Hello stranger, dear neighbor,
brave soldier, hey buddy,
I want you to know
we're glad you ate the goat meat
half-cooked over burning paper,
that you handed out jawbreakers,
that you researched the body
and all its invisible hinges:
the hair that melts and bones
that flavor the blood like soup,
thank you, we mean it,
for feeding one stray dog
but not the other,
for eating beef stew from a bag
and cocoa beverage powder
on your anniversary,
on Christmas,
thanks for drowning the mice
together in the same bucket,
for finding Sergeant Garcia first,
for bringing Connor home
and running the memorial race,
for dropping that rose
into the ground in Pennsylvania,
for wearing your blues,
you sure look sharp, you look good,
you wouldn't know you're a soldier,
you're such a normal guy,
thanks for trusting the interpreter,
for saying *woah, woah, woah*
and giving money to the sheikh,
thanks for giving your heavy knife

to the Afghan colonel as a gift,
for waiting to hear if the city fell,
thanks for going abroad, overseas,
into the sandbox, hell and back,
Godknowswhere and no-man's-land,
we can only imagine the PTSD,
the hopelessness, the sedatives, the sweats,
we're so happy you made it,
you survived, you came back,
not a dent in the fender,
this beer's for you, buddy, sir,
kiddo, without you
I wouldn't be free to drink it.

THANK YOU FOR YOUR SERVICE

You try a new response each time
and none of them work.
They strangle you like a belt,
right there at the grocery store
in front of the potato crate,
they choke you at the DMV,
smother you on the bike trail.

Today, when the veterinarian
shook your hand and wouldn't let go,
you called it a living and she said
It's so much more than that,
clapping her left hand over your knuckles.
The dog whined, smelling biscuits.

At home, we eat dinner on the porch steps,
plates on our knees and iced tea
glowing at our ankles like lanterns.
You tell me about Haditha Dam,
two boys from 82nd Airborne
dragged from their truck
and cut to pieces like goats by the road.

You shrug, say they'd fallen asleep,
headphones snug in their ears.
This is why music isn't allowed,
why forgetting where you are is lethal.

The pear tree in our yard,
the one that was here before us and flowers
with the stench of death each spring,
shakes itself out over the lumpy grass.
We let the dog roll in its rancid petals,
complain instead about the mosquitoes,
how they grow bigger every year.

HAPPY BIRTHDAY, ARMY

I'm wearing lace this time,
gold trim over a black slip because
Happy birthday, army!
I offer you these blisters
in my black leather stilettos
with mock-lace cut-outs.
Tom says it's a short ceremony,
we'll be done by nine
but he tells the sitter eleven
and I wedge a book into my purse.
In seeing nothing I've read too much:
the empty-bellied howitzer
kicked up in the corner of the ballroom
points me toward the cash bar,
casts a shadow over the cream
in my Kahlúa and turns the milk grey.
I drink it. I order a second
before the emcee tells the men
to seat their ladies.

Uniforms droop by the exits
on velvet hangers, gas masks
sag on wooden dowels.
Quick, boys! Post the colors!
The lights drop and the general
mounts the stage in a shimmer
of green and yellow spotlights,
tells us to enjoy ourselves for once—
but first these messages:
thank you to our guest speaker,
the anchor from ESPN,
thank you to our sponsors,

thank you to the sergeant major
here to recite "Old Glory"
in the center of the room:
I am arrogant.
I am proud.
I bow to no one.
I am worshipped.
We are dumbstruck,
the poem flung toward us
like an axe through paper.
Tom finds him later
and pays for his beer.

The chandeliers are champagne,
crystal brims sloshing with bubbles.
Someone's wife wins a kayak
and just when I think
a lieutenant nearby will surely jump
from his table to shake
a bag of limbs from his eye sockets,
a truckload of body parts
green with longing for the soul,
a woman's voice whispers
from beneath the howitzer,
the rented microphone
on fire with song:
Happy birrrthday, dear arrrmy
à la Marilyn Monroe,
and we are all a bunch of JFKs
in our lace and heels
and cummerbunds and cords.
We watch a five-tiered cake

piped in black and gold buttercream
being pulled between our tables
by a silver robot
and shrug into the silk of knowing
we could end all this
with the flick of a finger
if we wanted.

YOUR INTERPRETER SENDS ME A HOUSEDRESS

When you return to Iraq or Afghanistan
you are given new clothes as gifts:
the long robe made of goat fur which, even folded up,
is the size of a small desk. The brown turban,
the rough cotton tunic and pants.
We have photos of you sipping chai in these clothes,
sitting cross-legged in the sun. Your teeth shine
as you laugh with the Iraqi interpreter
who sits beside you holding bread in one hand.
When you leave he will be hunted by men
who come down from the hills at night
in white garments like stars crashing into Earth.
He will send you messages that say, *My brother*
until he is rescued by civilians
and sent to San Diego to work as a valet.
On your last day in Iraq, he gives you a housedress
in a plastic envelope and says it is a gift
for your wife: a woman who accepts gifts from men
other than her husband because she can,
because she does not know sending a dress to his wife
would be as unforgivable as touching her hair.
The dress is meant to be worn indoors:
orange and yellow with flashes of red,
the color of so many explosions I've watched on the news:
balloons of flame that float over mosques and markets.
At home, in our dining room, I pull the dress on
even though I am unaccustomed to its slim waist
and fussy gold thread, the zebra lamé pattern
stretched thin across my broad shoulders
and barreled chest, the Virgin Mary languishing
on a tin medallion under my throat.
I am too tall, too wide, and too plain for this dress,

too frank and impatient for its shimmering neckline
and narrow sleeves. I feel like I am smothering it.
We hang it on one of your good suit hangers
at the back of our closet where it smolders
and gleams between my wool sweaters and jeans,
throws sparks of light into my shoes.

THREE

THE AGE OF STRAYS

No one will tell us
we caused the problem,
wishing so often
during the pregnancy
when my bones
and blood ached,
wouldn't it be nice
if it were just a kitten.
Once, in the Starbucks
drive-through, you said
we could buy it
a hundred collars
for the price of a good stroller
and I said *maybe I'd gain*
ten pounds instead of fifty.
At the hospital in February
I barely gripped the handrails
of the delivery bed.
There were bits of mascara
on the doctor's paper face mask
when she said
it's a healthy male,
orange stripes, white paws.
Here is a woman
who sees all the earth
as a science exhibit,
who will not realize
until she writes it out
in ballpoint pen on a blue chart
that she has delivered us
from the Age of Strays.
She handed the cat

to a nurse to be swaddled
and placed on my chest.
You, my beloved,
stood hunched at my pillow,
staring at my socked feet
in the stirrups,
pointing at ten and two,
then at the cat, still slick
and beginning to howl,
swatting at the nurse.
You knew it was us
who had granted ourselves
one wish,
who had wanted,
at the very least,
a son.

POEM FOR BOYS

Nine years old and I thought boys
were the unlucky ones,
born with the tragic body part:
a disease they wore on the outside
like a barnacle or drooping fin.
On the bus after school, Andrew Martin
flung his hands over his zipper
when I stood up fast,
missed my stop by a mailbox.

I thought boys were a burden,
watched Colin cry in *The Secret Garden*
while Mary tore his shutters open,
heard my grandmother gripe about the boys
who became president, became traffic cops.
I expected greatness from boys
the way I expected it from jellyfish,
feared them as I feared seaweed, how it
washed up in knots with the driftwood.

When I was nine, boys
were an exercise in compassion
and I confessed to Father David
that I did not like them,
they were frail and impractical,
too much like roses.
Andrew Martin's mother told him
he could be anything he wanted
and I told Andrew she lied.

In my house, only girls
had the grit to transform themselves,

my mother's finger looped in gold
she bought herself.
When I was nine I told boys I could
breathe underwater and drew gills
behind my ears with permanent marker.
My teacher scrubbed and scrubbed.
I could taste the soap in my throat.

STOLLEN

My father was a blue whale.
He could outrun science and the doctors
with tools to chase him never knew
where he went for love.
No one knows what killed him.
When he turned up dead in his bathroom
he sprawled over the entire beach,
tiny white crabs pouring out of his mouth.
Blood on the bath mat was blood
in the kelp beds. He was carried away
like wood, emptied, cleaned
and sunk in a cheap blue casket.
He borrowed money from good, hungry men
at the junkyard and they followed him
like good, hungry fish.
A scientist from *National Geographic*
supposes the blue whale is not a phenomenon
but our tolerating its mystery is a marvel.
Because my father was a blue whale
he performed his miracles alone,
went to liquor stores alone
and filled prescriptions at Target alone.
He floated down the aisle of Band-Aids
with barnacles in every pocket.
People said, *would you look at that.*
When he was invited home for holidays,
I was old enough to know he was not wanted,
young enough to feel sorry.
He brought Stollen, the heavy bread nobody liked,
its tough crust hidden in sugar.
I taught myself carefully: *eat this bread.*
And I ate because my father was a blue whale

and Stollen was strange the way krill are strange.
I learned we could eat thousands of pounds
of Stollen in a single feeding,
there by the Christmas tree,
his heart the size of a taxicab idling in his ribs,
his backbone cutting the surface
of an ocean before he disappeared.

HOLIDAY

Today is National Vanilla Pudding Day
and everyone has pudding but you.
They eat it in their cars and in bed,
they serve it in the break room
where you find yesterday's scraps
of National Memo Day.
They wonder why you never celebrate.

Last year on National Save a Spider Day
you could find no living thing,
it was a Saturday and you searched
the coffee pot, your sink, the shower.

Today is National Buy a Musical Instrument Day
and you remember your mother at the music shop
cash register, renting the tiny violin that smelled
like sap and hot nickels. You want to go back
and buy the violin with newspaper money
or cookie cash but you're broke
even when you dream.

On National Waiter and Waitress Day
you slice your own apples and cheese,
pour milk over oat bran for dinner
and eat by the radiator, spinning the number wheel.

I'm writing to you now, friend, about tomorrow:
National Lucky Penny Day,
International Jazz Day.
Keep your eyes down on your way
to the bathroom for that secret cigarette,
breathe deep until the sprinkler spits to life
and Craig finds you soaked by the paper towels.

I want you to pull the silver whirls
of burning comfort into your lungs
like they're Sonny Rollins's last two breaths,
like it's National Turtle Day
and you've spent the past year
crawling from a hole in the ground
toward the California coast.

WHAT IS NAMED, WHAT IS UNNAMED

A man with a cleft palate
walks into the Pierce County DMV
and the woman who prints tickets
for us to hold while we wait says
Let's see some ID, which he doesn't have
but wants. His friend says something
in Pashtu, that much I know,
and the man nods, his front tooth
like the moon between curtains.
He wants identification, he wants
a ticket for every question he has,
he wants the woman to give him
a piece of paper with his picture on it.
So he gets back in line after she tells him
to sit down, getting louder each time: *Sir,*
she says, *we'll call you when we need you,*
and he nods again, wanting to please her,
which he must wait in line to do.
His friend says they are sorry,
they will sit. He bows. I can't watch.
My water bottle rolls off the chair
and a woman in desert camouflage
bolts an inch into the air like a cat,
glares at me like the weapon I am.
This is strike two: she knows I've been
reading the *Times* over her shoulder.
NASA is revisiting Pluto, which
has done well since its unnaming,
its mountains draped in sexy veils
of shadow we can hardly stand.
The woman rolls the paper and feigns
disinterest in what New York has to say

about the universe, which chunks of space
are worth wanting or identifying,
which planets inch closer and which ones turn
with indifference, their faces lined with scars
we remember so well in photographs.

HOW TO VISIT A GRAVE PROPERLY

Four years after the burial
I take the red-eye
from New York to Seattle
and drive a rented Hyundai
to the Tacoma Boys grocery,
a business he would have ignored
with its European cheeses
and Nutella pyramid.
Walla Walla sweet onions
are a buck apiece.
I know an Italian grandmother
who says she never shows up
anywhere without a gift
so I'm going to bring my dad
this sweet onion
in its faded pinstripes
even if it won't be eaten
the way he liked them,
sliced and salted,
dropped in a cereal bowl.
I drive into Auburn,
I mean really into Auburn
over the Green River
where a man once buried women
in the moss like bulbs.
At the Tahoma National Cemetery
a kiosk points me toward gravesite 28A,
the most affordable plot
we could find on short notice.
I stand there with the onion.
It's a little soft near the root.
Dad, you never taught me
how to visit a grave properly

so I've brought you this onion
in the middle of August
when it's going to bake
out here in the open
and stink the place up.
I feel sorry for your gravemates
if that's what they're called,
the soldiers buried around you
whose families call them
good fathers and God's servant.
I feel sorry for you too,
down there in your Christmas sweater
even though you left a suit
laid out on the bed.
We dressed you in Irish wool
the way your mother did.
The onion sinks into your new yard
like a bird's egg. It looks good,
glowing like manners
bundled in the sun.
Suppose my thoughts as I stood there
counted as prayer.
Suppose I spent the moment
wishing for salt.

MOTHERHOOD IS NOT ENOUGH FOR ME

At the OBGYN a framed portrait
  of my uterus hangs in the lobby:
    the flabby petals of a wilted iris,

eggs bunched up like bees in the clouds.
  This is not the garden where I'll be saved.
  Motherhood is not enough for me

even though it expands in the stomach
  like bread and dries the skin like salt.
  My daughter came into the world

as if she was voted into power
  fair and square, an election held
    in the private booth of my brain stem

after years of suppression.
  Now that I have my own baby
    it is safe to invite me to baby showers

and feed me tiny sandwiches
  and ask about my breast pump
    while the world burns down outside.

I wanted her, I do, but I wouldn't say
  I trust her, not really, not the way
    she builds herself beyond me now

with her own materials.
  Here is what it comes to:
    motherhood is not enough for me

even when I swallow it like cake,
  even when I wipe my mouth
    on a napkin emblazoned with its flag.

INTERNATIONAL WOMEN'S DAY

The world observes my sex
on the same day America
celebrates the pancake,
and who doesn't love a good pancake?
There is no such thing
as celebrating myself.
This is the sound of cards
being stacked, the odds lined up
against my house like firewood.
This year, for International Women's Day,
I read the newspaper when I should be
warming milk slow on the stove
for my daughter
or dressing her in school clothes
or mailing a letter
or skipping the newspaper:
Death Valley, it seems, is heavy
with wildflowers after a series
of unexpected storms,
its basin shimmering
with blooms that must be named
after racehorses: desert gold,
burgundy five-spot,
brown-eyed evening primrose
and the silky gravel ghost.
This is not a poem.
The grass in my backyard
does not rejoice in solidarity,
its salutations shushed
by a South Sound wind.
We've set aside entire days
to remember what we forget
and forget what we know:

there is no better name for privilege,
no party for the fat wallet
or the lucky heir,
the pale cheek with facial hair.
Scientists in Death Valley
can't say how long these seeds
have waited for rain,
but the answer is written in red:
longer than a year.

WHAT TO ASK FOR

Four weeks post-partum
and I ask for a knife
I can strap to my seat belt.
For river crossings, I say,
because we live in Binghamton
and it's March and I drive
over the Susquehanna
at least twice a day,
the ice that groans
between me and drowning.
A knife feels smooth
against the gut of fear:
my daughter and I dropping
like eggs from a bird's nest
off the collapsed bridge,
her car seat clips jammed,
my forehead tossed
against the windshield.
I ask for a life hammer.
I ask just in case.
I ask for sleeping pills
that won't seep into breastmilk
because even when I sink
I want to lift this child
over my head to safety.
Tom brings a claw-shaped blade
home from work in a green sheath.
He fastens it to the buckle
beside my center console
and stows an orange hammer
in my door, shows me how
to shield my eyes and swing.

When the doctor discovers
a safe way for me to sleep,
I dream I am so young
my eyes have not decided
what color they will be.

HAIL AND FAREWELL AS A JUNKYARD DOG

The colonel and his wife
are being sent to Fort Hood.
At their Hail and Farewell
I sit in the corner, a junkyard dog
on the overstuffed armchair.
The captain's wife asks me
if by going back to school
I will become a real doctor
or just the kind that writes.
Because I am a dog, I growl.
I do unladylike things:
show my teeth when I smile,
answer to my own whistle.
The conversation turns to childbirth,
labor stories, and breastfeeding.
Because I am a dog,
I don't say much.
I pretend someone's called for me
and pace at the window
where I have a good view
of the men by the firepit.
They drink PBR from the can.
They could be anyplace.
I pray for them to wave me outside,
to share their potato chips.
But the major's wife shoos them inside
for the formal ceremony.
The colonel receives a plaque.
His wife gets a rose I recognize
from the rubber buckets at Chevron.
Everyone is excited about Texas.

I sit next to my husband
who is not a junkyard dog,
who smiles like he means it.
He places one finger
on the soft spot behind my ear
and I can hear his skin
telling me I've been so good.

MY DAUGHTER PRACTICES SAYING HI

This is how she lulls herself to sleep
in the portable crib she has outgrown,
and even if I didn't want to listen
I would hear her now, in summer,
when the house leans downhill
and the bedroom door will not shut.
Between her and me, two bookcases
bulge with poems, their shelves
bowed like ribs. Between her and me
are a thousand songs. Daughter,
my last words to you each night say
only that I am nearby, and that means
your voice is a quarter-moon in my window:
you say *Hi!* then wait for me to answer.
I've gone downstairs to close curtains,
pour water into the coffee pot,
fold clothes we will unfold in the morning.
You say *Hi!* again and again,
happy to meet yourself there
between the collapsible poles of your bed,
the fitted blue sheet and stuffed elephant
with a bow sewn onto one ear.
Because it is June, because the house
has pulled away from winter as if to complain,
as if to say she has raised many daughters,
because the moon crests our stairwell
through a window so high I cannot cover it,
because I am close by and you are awake,
I listen to you practice saying *Hi!*
in all its forms: welcome, I know you,
here I am, come in, I've missed you.

HOW TO COMFORT A SMALL CHILD

advice I've found and received

Wallpaper the living room
with a world map.
Put a green thumbtack
through Fort Carson,
a red tack through Kandahar.
Buy stuffed bears
dressed in camouflage and dog tags,
sew a recording of dad's voice
into the bear's chest
where its heart should be.
Have him read stories
or recite prayers.
Spell out certain words
on the phone: d-e-a-d,
m-i-s-s-i-n-g, w-o-u-n-d-e-d.
Be organized. Make lists.
Children want to see order,
they need to see you sad
but not too sad.
Keep busy. Keep a journal.
Make daddy dolls
and daddy pillows.
If it is economically feasible,
print a life-size cutout
of dad with arms spread wide.
Children can hug cutouts
and photographs.
Try yoga. Try karate.
Build memory boxes
and fill them with sentimental items,

an old watch or clean t-shirt.
Build picture frames.
Build scrapbooks.
Projects that require building
give children a sense of purpose.
Limit the family's exposure
to news programs.
Expect children to ask
about torture and ransom,
topics beyond their years.
Use words they understand.
Express love. Try fun outings:
days at the zoo
and movies in the park.
Be joyful. Don't dwell.
Read articles written for moms.
Avoid taking on added responsibilities
such as job promotions,
transfers, or school programs.
Try cocoa, try jellybeans, try gum.
Write brief letters.
Ask the Red Cross.
Ask your doctor.
Ask to speak with the principal.
Make friends with women
who understand, women
with children and spouses
who haven't called in days.
When your daughter
flushes her plastic fox
down the toilet
and says he went to Afghanistan,
don't read into it.
Call a plumber.

PHANTOM LIMB

You say it is amazing what Afghans can build
with so little, and I picture them approaching your outpost
at night like gods who have been summoned,
shaken loose from the mountains.
They unravel coils of metal wrapped around gravel
and earth: Hesco bastions meant to absorb shrapnel.
They take wires away wound around their arms
elbow to shoulder, and the next morning you find a fence
with a swinging gate staked around the patch
of watermelon vines so beautiful it reminds you of home.
You say they can build anything if they are given
enough wire, the hood of a car, a curtain, some water.
Across the ocean, I know I am not a builder.
I've hammered myself into your side,
useful as a phantom limb. I see everything you see
and do nothing except remind you where you left me.

CALLING RATS

In the desert, in a concrete hut
with a door made of cloth,
a rat gives birth in the filing cabinet
containing your last two t-shirts.
She shreds the collars for comfort,
surrounds her brood with the gnashed threads
of your clothing and nests herself
in the scent of your neck torn to ribbons.
Into a bucket of water they go.
When you tell the story a year later
you slump at our kitchen table,
a houseplant blooming with blame.
War brought the rats to me, you say,
they stole the last bit of cotton
between my body and the burn pit.
At night I open your eyelids and see the rat,
her children asleep in your skull.
When I coax them out they do not trust me.
I offer them some paper, a piece of apple.
They want the hem of your sleeve.

THE FALLING BODY

When our daughter falls
down the carpeted hotel stairs,

her body translates to others
you've seen before,

fingers outstretched in search of anchor,
elbows locked into columns.

You didn't catch those bodies
either, not even a sleeve.

She howls. You scream for me
the way a medic screamed for you,

yelling as if I don't kneel
on the same carpet you cradle her on,

its red lotus design bursting
like fire at night.

We lean into each other like ruins
beneath a glittering chandelier,

our backs to the guests
who line up to check out.

LUNCH AT THE WAR COLLEGE

We pull into the parking lot
at your next duty station,
the War College hunched like an old goat
in the crust of its own island.
A seagull drops to the asphalt
beside our car with a crab in its mouth,
smashes it against the curb
and digs in through the belly.

Nice girls don't ask
where you've brought them
and they don't believe in omens.
I ask how war is taught
at the college level and you say
it's not that simple.

Nice girls don't bring up
Ranger School graduation at parties,
how one lieutenant got tangled
on the zip-line and had to hang there
until the ceremony was over,
rifle strapped to his ribcage
and gum in his mouth.

Nice girls don't ask
if they're real knives or rubber
when you wrestle your brothers
with blades in a mock battle
while your parents and wives
watch in their church clothes.
None of us think
this is what it will look like
the moment our boy is killed.

We fattened you up for war,
let the army pick you up
like a turkey in winter, upside down,
let it drag you into the barn.

Nice girls promise
not to ask questions
when you return from the desert,
they promise to hold the cat
all the way from New York to Newport.

Nice girls ask
if we are lost when a deserted lot
looks nothing like the O Club,
nice girls ignore the scavenging birds.
They don't say *give me the map,*
they don't say *I'll find us.*

When we arrived at the War College
I snatched the map from your hands
and the seagull outside the car took off,
heavy with lunch,
the crab still waving one pincer
as if to say it wasn't hurt, wasn't dying.

MAKING COFFEE

An abandoned building burns down
six blocks away and we are up
at four to close windows,
witness the neighborhood
sleep through the ash.
The newspaper is already here.
It is 2016. We make coffee,
certain even Neruda made coffee
the morning he knew
he must sing to the air, beg her
not to sell herself like water.
We sit in the kitchen and drink,
a carton of cream between us.
Surely God made coffee
just after the first apple fell,
sat and pretended to be at peace
while Michael reached for the sword.

NATIONAL LIPSTICK DAY

Today I celebrate National Lipstick Day
by throwing my once-used six-year-old tube
of *Dallas Red* into the bathroom trash can

while the news anchor, a woman with a law degree
whose favorite shade is *Nude Beach,*
tells my empty living room that orange hues

make the teeth appear yellow while pink
widens the smile, and, according to neuroscientists in Britain,
a wider smile connotes the more approachable female.

By approachable they mean *a woman*
more likely to help than hinder. I call Tom at the War College
where he is not thinking about lipstick or smiling.

Newsprint rustles in the background like a bird,
a male species of news, news I sneak like a drug:
Gaza and its rocket tossing over the desert,

small stars thrown from one grey mitt of smoke to another.
Fact: there are more children in Iraq than explosives.
Stories of war find Tom like lost pups, blind and sniffing,

while I am trapped in the teeth of summer diet tricks
and nine sex moves that will keep Tom faithful.
This morning at Quick Lube, a TV near the ceiling told me

without knowing who I am what it thinks I need to know:
Kate Middleton uses her face to express emotions
at sporting events, her signature hand-over-mouth.

Lady Gaga tattooed Tony Bennett's family name on her arm.
In local news, a four-year-old girl from Broome County
drew a picture of the weather and won a grocery store coupon.

In it, she made globs of rain as big as the people
they fell on: her mom and herself without bodies,
two faces balanced on five-toed stilts.

HOW WE EAT

Tom eats well because the general eats well
and where the general goes Tom goes too,
armed only with blazers and briefcases.
I imagine lobster tails and prosciutto forks,
lemon wheels and wedges of cake served
under a silver cloche. I imagine rum and Coke
poured behind the first-class curtain.
For twelve months, Tom is home but not *home,*
he is here but gone, I am lonely but not alone.
I keep pepper spray in the nightstand
and read about cat-friendly booby traps.
I have the look of someone who stuns easy
and says little: men at the bus stop offer me
space under their umbrella, the time, a cut in line.
My sister calls to ask what I am eating and I tell her
I celebrate myself with plastic tumblers of pinot noir
and low-fat yogurt, quesadillas, peppers
and sliced apples served on takeout napkins.
For every roadside bomb not planted near the Pentagon
I bury another bulb of store-bought garlic that reached
with green arms toward my coffee pot:
shrine of the morning, my burbling priestess.
I honor isolation by not knitting blankets
or painting my daughter's name over her crib.
I stack books instead, stack bills and dishes
and flyers from the military bank that say
absence causes stress I can minimize by following
four easy steps: get a job, sharpen my skills,
identify my strengths, consider my location.
I work at the university where units of measurement
are made and I dull the blade of strategy
on the grit of a thousand red bricks.
Where I am is unclear. Every city looks like the city

I lived in two cities ago. At night the library windows
glow like summer chardonnay and I am closer
to eating a poem now than I ever was in college,
that first apartment we rented when Iraq was heating up
and the army gave Tom money for books
but we spent it on food, spaghetti and pancake mix,
meals we could prepare with water
and little else: the lidless pot, a pinch of salt.

HOW CAN I TELL YOU THIS?

I stepped outside with coffee
and dragged steam
from the lip of the mug,
all our grass dried to a pale non-color
and gnarled like the bones of birds
I don't recall falling.

How can I tell you,
when my daughter found a dead swallow
under the window at my mother's house,
we painted thin white loops on the glass
to keep its brothers from crushing
their handsome heads?
We put a dish of water out
for the stray Siamese,
we left pinecones dipped in peanut butter
and birdseed tied to the fencepost,
we buried a mama raccoon
I assumed had been dead for days.

How can I tell? Empty black pockets sagged
where the eyes once rolled.
Mornings come with news:
red flowers have opened
beneath a man's white t-shirt
and I want to tell my daughter
the burning petals aren't hers or mine,
but how can I?

Xavier, the man who planted Jonagolds
in our backyard, says the apples
will survive July's heat
but I don't see how they can.

They're just babies,
no bigger than birds' eggs,
they cling to the branches like snails
and this year fewer white flowers came.

How can I tell you this?
They say you can't put apples in a poem
without conjuring original sin
but I'm invoking knowledge here.
Take my apples and help me
warn my daughter that her chest
is full of red flowers I've put there
in hopes they never bloom.

SITTING IN A SIMULATED LIVING SPACE
AT THE SEATTLE IKEA

This is how you might arrange your life
if you were to start from scratch:
a newer, better version of yourself applied
coat by coat, beginning with lamplight
from the simulated living room.
The man who lives here has never killed.
There is no American camouflage drying
over the backs of his kitchen chairs,
no battle studies on the coffee table.
He travels without a weapon,
hangs photographs of the Taj Mahal,
the Eiffel Tower above the sofa.
The woman who lives here has no need
for prescriptions or self-help,
her mirror cabinet holds a pump
for lotion and a rose-colored water glass,
her nightstand is stacked with hardcovers
on Swedish architecture.
To sit in the simulated living space at Ikea
is to know what sand knows
as it rests inside the oyster.
The cat who lives here has been declawed,
the dog rehomed. There are no parakeets
shrilling over newspaper in the decorative cage,
no parking tickets in the breadbox.
When you finish your dollar coffee
and exit through the simulated front door,
join other shoppers with chapsticks
in their purses and Kleenex and receipts,
with t-shirts that say Florida Keys 2003
and unopened Nicorette in their pockets,

you wish you could say this place
is not enough for you, that you're better off
in the harsh light of the parking garage,
a light that shows your skin beneath your skin,
the color of your past self,
pale in places, flushed in others.

ACKNOWLEDGEMENTS

I am grateful to the editors who published my poems, sometimes
in differing form, in the following journals:

"The Age of Strays" and "A Portable Wife" *december*
"Bones" *Georgetown Review*
"Crossing the Knik" *Rhino*
"Five Days after the Wedding" *River Styx*
"Hail and Farewell" *New Letters*
"How to Be Married after Iraq" *Academy of American Poets*
"How We Eat" *Stone Canoe*
"Memorial Day" *Rattle: Poets Respond*
"My Daughter Practices Saying Hi" *All We Can Hold: Poems of
    Motherhood*
"Notification" and "Skin Lady" *Ragazine*
"Ode to Norteño" *The New Guard*
"Phantom Limb" and "Prayer on National Childfree Day" *Rattle*
"Poem for My Dog" and "Poem for Ugly People" *The Paterson
    Literary Review*
"Poem for Pregnant Women Who Hold Their Stomachs in
    Pictures" *Crosswinds*
"Rearview Mirror" *Cimarron Review*
"Shortly before the World Ended" *Confrontation*
"Sitting in a Simulated Living Space at the Seattle Ikea" *New
    Ohio Review*
"Stollen" *Crab Creek Review*
"Thank You for Your Service" *AWP Intro Journals Project*
"When He Receives Orders to Afghanistan and a Parking Ticket:
    How to Respond" *Dialogist*
"Why Women Write Poems for Their Sons" *Radar*

Note: The poems "Phantom Limb" (page 79) and "Calling Rats"
(page 80) were originally written in German by the author and then
translated into English by the author.

Hail and Farewell is a reimagining of my doctoral dissertation, and it would not have come together without the writers I met at Binghamton University, including Maria Gillan, Rosmarie Morewedge, Joe Weil, Nicole Santalucia, Dante Di Stefano, and Heather Dorn. Before Binghamton, I studied at Pacific University, where Marvin Bell, Dorianne Laux, Joe Millar, Ellen Bass, and the late Peter Sears were instrumental in keeping my writing, and me, alive.

Amy Murray and Kim Kusick have listened to me fume and rave through each permanent change of station, from cities in Alaska, Georgia, Colorado, New York, Rhode Island, and Washington. They visited often, helping me through infertility and rage, then pregnancy and motherhood. I'll never be done thanking them.

Thank you to my Poem Friday group, who let me write with abandon on a weekly basis, especially LeAnne Laux-Bachand, whose feedback is steady and kind. I'm grateful to spouses of service members who stuck around to listen and showed up for me: Andria Williams, Jeanie Chastain, Stephanie Rush, Moira Neal, and my friends around Joint Base Lewis-McChord. Thank you to my students, everywhere, who continue to make me stop what I'm doing and write.

My husband's experiences in the military and in combat have influenced my career as a poet and teacher. He operates in a culture that doesn't truly see me, and he has struggled, mostly with success, to question that. He has been there for me, as I have been for him. Here's to the rest of our lives, pal.

Thank you to Rebecca Olander and my Perugia Press family, whose fierce warmth and commitment to supporting women astonish and thrill me. They've seen me in my poems, and I'm forever grateful.

ABOUT THE AUTHOR

Abby E. Murray completed her MFA at Pacific University and her Ph.D. in English at SUNY Binghamton, where this book was written. She's taught creative writing at high school and university levels and currently teaches argumentative writing to U.S. Army War College fellows sent to the University of Washington. Abby is the editor of *Collateral*, a literary journal concerned with the impact of violent conflict and military service beyond the combat zone, and as the 2019–2021 poet laureate for the city of Tacoma, Washington, she offers free poetry workshops around Pierce County, including at military posts and detention centers for undocumented youth. This is her first book.

ABOUT PERUGIA PRESS

Perugia Press publishes one collection of poetry each year, by a woman at the beginning of her publishing career. Our mission is to produce beautiful books that interest long-time readers of poetry and welcome those new to poetry. We also aim to celebrate and promote poetry whenever we can, and to keep the cultural discussion of poetry inclusive.

Also from Perugia Press:

➤ *Girldom,* Megan Peak
➤ *Starshine Road,* L. I. Henley
➤ *Brilliance, Spilling: Twenty Years of Perugia Press Poetry*
➤ *Guide to the Exhibit,* Lisa Allen Ortiz
➤ *Grayling,* Jenifer Browne Lawrence
➤ *Sweet Husk,* Corrie Williamson
➤ *Begin Empty-Handed,* Gail Martin
➤ *The Wishing Tomb,* Amanda Auchter
➤ *Gloss,* Ida Stewart
➤ *Each Crumbling House,* Melody S. Gee
➤ *How to Live on Bread and Music*, Jennifer K. Sweeney
➤ *Two Minutes of Light,* Nancy K. Pearson
➤ *Beg No Pardon*, Lynne Thompson
➤ *Lamb*, Frannie Lindsay
➤ *The Disappearing Letters*, Carol Edelstein
➤ *Kettle Bottom*, Diane Gilliam Fisher
➤ *Seamless*, Linda Tomol Pennisi
➤ *Red*, Melanie Braverman
➤ *A Wound On Stone*, Faye George
➤ *The Work of Hands*, Catherine Anderson
➤ *Reach*, Janet E. Aalfs
➤ *Impulse to Fly*, Almitra David
➤ *Finding the Bear*, Gail Thomas

The text of this book is set in Monotype Century Schoolbook, a variant of the Century type family that was designed by Linn Boyd Benton in 1894 for master printer Theodore Low De Vinne for use in *The Century Magazine*, one of the most popular magazines in the United States in its heyday in the 1880s. At the request of textbook publisher Ginn and Company, Century Schoolbook was designed in 1919 by Benton's son, Morris Fuller Benton, with an emphasis on elegant simplicity and legibility suitable for young readers. The classic type design has endured through hot metal, photomechanical, and digital typesetting.

The poem titles are set in Clarendon, designed in London in 1845 by Robert Besley and released by Thorowgood and Co. The type, characterized by its boldness, legibility, and square serifs, spawned an entire classification of headline types with the same design properties. Its strength and legibility have made it an enduring typeface for poster design, signage, and other display uses.